Physical Activity Right From the Start

What Parents Can Do During the First 5 Years

Steve Sanders

TeachingStrategies® | Washington, D.C.

The publisher and the authors cannot be held responsible for injury, mishap, or damages incurred during the use of or because of the information in this book. The authors recommend appropriate and reasonable supervision at all times based on the age and capability of each child.

Editor: Toni Bickart
Cover Design and Layout: Abner Nieves
Illustrations: Anthony LeTourneau
Spanish Edition Translation: Alicia Fontán

Teaching Strategies, Inc.
P.O. Box 42243
Washington, DC 20015
www.TeachingStrategies.com
800-637-3652

ISBN: 978-1-60617-393-0

First Printing: 2011

Library of Congress Cataloging-in-Publication Data

Sanders, Steve.
  Physical activity right from the start : what parents can do in the first 5 years / Steve Sanders.
    p. cm.
  ISBN 978-1-60617-393-0
  1. Physical education for children. 2. Early childhood education--Parent participation. I. Title.
  GV443.S195 2011
  372.86--dc23
                                        2011036726

Printed and bound in the United States of America

Contents

Introduction

Do you know that you can help your child...

enjoy physical activity?

feel good about his or her physical skills?

use physical skills to solve problems?

feel confident when playing with friends?

live a healthier life?

Physical activity is a big part of your child's life. Every time you and your child take a walk, gallop down the sidewalk, or throw and catch a ball together, you are helping your child develop physical skills. The early years are an important time for young children to learn these skills, which they will use every day as they play and move. When you help your child practice and use physical skills, your child becomes stronger, healthier, and more confident.

Learning basic physical skills is essential for your child's healthy growth and development. Sadly, an increasing number of children in the U.S. are obese today. This alarming situation is due in large part to unhealthy eating habits and the fact that too many children are not physically active. Children who are overweight are more likely to develop serious health problems as they grow older.

Strong physical skills don't just develop effortlessly. Children need lots of practice and support. As their physical skills improve, their strength and self-confidence grow. When children discover what their bodies can do, they are able to learn new physical skills more easily. They also learn more about their environment and the world, which will help them become more creative and more successful in school. All of these wonderful traits will make it more likely that children will be physically active and therefore lead healthier lives as adults.

Throughout your day, look for opportunities to be physically active and play with your child. Whether you walk to the park, play on playground equipment, ride bikes, or move to music, you can find ways to have fun and be active with your child. You don't need to buy special toys or fancy equipment; an old rolled-up sock makes a great ball to throw and catch! You don't need to be an expert to be physically active, either.

This book shows you how you can support your child's natural interest in being physically active and learning new skills. You'll see how much you can already do, and you'll learn new games to play. By choosing the activities both you and your child enjoy most, you'll have fun being physically active together and you'll help your child build a solid foundation for a healthy lifestyle.

Helping Your Child Be Physically Active

It may seem like a challenge at first to help your child learn about physical activity. However, there are many fun and easy ways to help your child learn basic physical skills. *Physical activity* simply means moving your body in a healthy way. Any time you play with your child, take a walk in the park, throw a ball, dance, or swim, you are being physically active. When your child sees you participating in physical activity, he will be more likely to choose to be active later in life.

The first 5 years of your child's life are important because this is when she is developing basic physical skills. Your child will not always learn these skills on her own, so this is the time to provide her with lots of opportunities for physical activity and skill development. She'll need your help to learn and practice challenging activities.

Your child should be physically active for several hours each day—but not all at once. Instead, throughout the day, try to have short periods of activity for 15–20 minutes at a time. Young children need rest breaks.

Ways We Move

As children experiment with movement and practice physical skills, they learn how to control their bodies for a purpose. They learn how close to place their bodies to objects and people, how slowly or quickly to move, and how much strength it takes to do a particular activity. As they learn to plan and coordinate their movements, children build their knowledge about what are often called *movement concepts*.

Here are some examples of activities that help children learn about movement concepts:

- Moving in a large space without bumping into people or things
- Pointing to and identifying different body parts
- Creating different shapes with the body, including wide, narrow, curved, round, or twisted shapes
- Traveling over, under, around, and through obstacles on a playground
- Throwing balls to see how far they will travel
- Comparing how high and how far different balls travel when you throw them
- Drawing straight, curved, and zigzag lines on paper, and then moving in those ways
- Tiptoeing across a room
- Moving forward, backward, and sideways

Traveling Skills

When infants are around 3 months old, they begin turning over by themselves. Soon, they will crawl, walk, run, leap, hop, jump, gallop, and skip. They will use these traveling skills to move from place to place. Learning these skills helps children explore and discover their world. One of the best ways for you to help your child learn traveling skills is to show the skill first. "Follow me! Look, we're galloping!" "Let's jump over the crack in the sidewalk and land on both feet. I'll go first. Let me show you."

Here are some other ways to practice traveling skills with your child:

- Explore ways to move while pretending to be different types of animals.
- Walk, run, or gallop in large open spaces while holding hands.
- Walk or run around objects.
- Walk forward and backward.
- Bend your elbows and swing your arms as you run.
- Climb across playground equipment.
- Hold one foot in the air as you hop up and down on the other.
- Jump and land on two feet.

Balance Skills

Your child uses balance to control his body every day. Your child uses one kind of balance skill when he freezes like a statue or balances on one leg without moving. Your child uses another kind of balance skill to walk across a low balance beam without falling or to keep control of his body when he rolls down a hill. Good balance skills help your child move safely without falling during physical activity.

Here are some ways to practice balance skills:

- Balance on different body parts, creating different shapes with the body.

- Hold a position for 5 seconds without moving.

- Balance on different objects, such as a balance beam or other playground equipment.

- Stop moving and remain balanced without falling.

- Extend body parts outward to assist in balancing.

- Travel across a low beam without falling off.

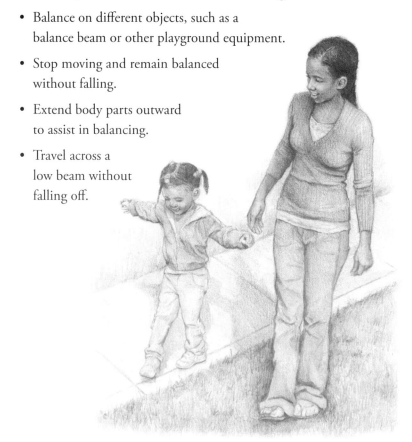

Ball Skills

Your child will love to play with balls. Ball skills include throwing, catching, collecting, kicking, punting, dribbling, and volleying, as well as striking with paddles, rackets, and sticks with long handles—such as bats and hockey sticks. Children of all ages like to find balls and watch them bounce, spin, roll, and fly through the air. Play a ball game with your child as often as you can.

Here are some ways to practice ball skills:

- Kick a ball while standing still.
- Catch a rolling ball.
- Hit a light ball into the air.
- Bounce a ball and catch it.
- Throw with one hand while stepping with the opposite foot.
- Kick by using the top of your foot.
- Keep your eyes on the ball when attempting to catch it.
- Dribble a ball, using your fingertips.

Creating a Safe Place for Physical Activity

When you provide a safe place at home for physical activity, you help your child become physically active. Try to be available to help your child when she is practicing physical skills. Here are some ways to encourage more physical activity at home.

Identify places where your child can play and explore. Remove any objects in the way. Make a comfortable space.

Create a place where you and your child can move freely and safely. When being active indoors, be sure to move dangers out of the way, like glass mirrors, floor lamps, furniture, sharp edges, and breakable items. Cover electrical outlets, close doors and drawers that can pinch, and close off open stairways. Also be sure that your child's clothing will not limit movement.

Play on carpeted floors. Wood or tile floors can be slippery.

Provide a place to put balls, beanbags, scarves, and musical instruments. Put them in boxes and mark each one with a picture of the object.

Play your child's favorite music in the background. Have an assortment of music and songs that encourage your child to move and dance.

Find out about the weather before you go outside. Dress appropriately so you and your child will be comfortable. If it is very hot or too cold, you may not want to be outside.

When outside, find a large, open space. Look for a flat area with no holes to step into or things to trip over.

Make sure equipment is properly made for your child. Be sure that it is the right size for your child and fits her skill level. Do not use equipment made for adults. Provide equipment that is lightweight and made for young children. Do not use equipment with rough or sharp edges. Check that the equipment is clean and replace it when it breaks. When possible, choose brightly colored equipment.

Helping Your Child Develop Physical Skills

Parents play an important role in helping their children develop physical skills. You are your child's first and lifelong teacher. Here are some important ways to help your child develop physical skills.

Plan activities that are fun. Help your child have fun and be successful. Plan activities your child will enjoy and can successfully complete about 80 percent of the time. If she gets frustrated because she cannot hit a target, then have her move closer to it. If he is bored because he hits a target every time, then encourage him to move farther away. When an activity is too hard or too easy, your child may not enjoy it and may have a more difficult time learning new skills.

Encourage your child to explore. Be positive! No matter what your child's skill level is, you can always say encouraging things. Your child needs to try, practice, and explore different movements before he's ready to hear how to do it the "right" way. If you want to work with your child on kicking a ball, for example, give him a ball outside in a large area. Tell him to do what he wants with the ball. As he plays, you will be able to see where he needs help and give tips for improvement. After watching your child play for a while, you might say, "Wait until the ball stops rolling before you kick it again," or say, "Kick with the side of your foot instead of with your toes." Explore first and then provide specific instructions when your child is ready.

Create challenging activities. Your child will need lots of practice to improve her physical skills. A challenge can make the practice more fun. Try asking your child to do the activity in a different way. Instead of saying, "Throw a beanbag and hit the target," you might ask, "Can you hit the target three times in a row?" Instead of asking, "Can you bounce the ball?" you might ask, "How many times can you bounce the ball with one hand?" Remember that children love to copy what adults do. For instance, you might challenge your child to see whether she can stand on one foot longer than you can. Suggest, "Let's see who can balance on one foot longer!"

Be physically active with your child. Show your child that physical activity is important. Plan some time each day to play with your child. You might take a walk, go to the park, or play in the yard. The more your child practices with you, the more he will enjoy his new skills.

Giving Your Baby a Good Start

How can my child be physically active? He's just a baby.
He's not ready to throw, catch, or kick a ball, but he likes to
crawl and wants to put everything in his mouth. What should
I do to encourage development of physical skills?

Babies learn a lot about their bodies and new spaces as they move around. Even though your baby may not yet be rolling, throwing, catching, or kicking, there's so much you can do and say to help him learn how his body can move. By the end of the first year, your baby will start to gain control of his body. He discovers his feet. He reaches with his hands to touch and place objects in his mouth. He lifts his head and rolls over. He may scoot backward on his back and creep forward on his belly. He laughs and screams with delight when he discovers the new things he can do with his body.

Your baby is just beginning her journey! She is learning to sit up and can watch bubbles flying through the air. She grasps things in her hands, and she can drop or propel things into the air. She will soon crawl, pull up on furniture to stand, and take her first steps. She is learning about all the ways her body can move. With these skills, your baby is ready to make discoveries about physical activity.

You can help! Make time for physical play with your child—about 10–15 minutes, four or five times each day. Together, touch and hold objects of different sizes and textures, including various balls to roll and push. Ask, "Does this feel hard or soft?" Sing, sway back and forth, and move his body to the beat of the music.

Name parts of his body as you touch them. "Is this your nose? Yes! That's your nose." "Is that your finger? How many fingers do you have?" You might also say, "These are your hands," or ask, "Can you touch your toes?" As you play, you might say, "I'm going to tickle your belly!"

You can even help your child learn about balance when you rock back and forth with him. You can strengthen your child's muscles by gently rolling him over and over on a soft mat or on the carpet. Each time you play with him, you help him develop the skills he needs to be physically active and let him know that physical activity is fun.

Ways Your Baby Moves

A young baby might…

- Follow your movement with his eyes as you walk across the room.
- Reach into the air to catch and pop bubbles.
- Smile and laugh as you play peek-a-boo.
- Clap his hands together and touch his toes.

An older baby might…

- Push or pull toys.
- Bang sticks and musical instruments together to make noise.
- Crawl around objects or through tunnels.
- Track a ball that rolls across the floor.

Ways Your Baby Moves		
If you...	and say...,	your child will begin to...
talk to your baby as you move from one place to another in the room	"Can you see me?" "Here I am!"	learn to lift her head, track objects in space, and understand movement in different directions.
blow bubbles with your baby	"Look at the bubbles!" "Let's pop them!" "Can you catch a bubble?"	follow the movement of objects and develop catching skills.
put the corner of a soft blanket loosely on your baby's face and then quickly remove it	"Peek-a-boo, I see you!" "Now *you* pull it off."	understand the concepts of *on* and *off*.
touch or tickle different parts of your baby's body (her feet, head, knees, back, etc.)	"This is your foot!" "Can you touch your ears?" "Where is Mommy's nose?"	learn the names of body parts, and understand how they move and what they do.
talk to your baby as you move him from place to place	"Now we are moving up." "Let's go forward." "Let's go backward."	understand direction.
play with drums, sticks, pots, pans, and wooden spoons	"Hit the pan hard with the spoon!" "Now play a soft song!" "Play the drum as fast as you can!"	understand the ideas of *hard* and *soft*, *fast*, and *slow*.

Traveling Skills

A young baby might…

- Stretch and extend his arms to reach toward you or for objects.
- Turn her head to the sound of your voice.
- Kick as though he is riding a bicycle when lying on his back.
- Reach her hands to play with her feet.
- Creep forward on his belly.

An older baby might…

- Pull herself up to stand.
- Crawl quickly across the room and around furniture.
- Cruise or walk, holding onto furniture.
- Begin to take his first steps.

Promoting Your Baby's Traveling Skills

If you...	and say...,	your child will begin to...
lay your child on his belly and place toys in front of him	"Can you get the toy?"	strengthen back and neck muscles that support his head, and reach and move forward.
place your baby on her belly in front of a mirror	"Who's that?"	lift her head, and strengthen her neck muscles so she can control the movement of her head.
put a toy slightly out of your baby's reach, moving it a little further away as he moves closer	"Can you get the block?"	try to crawl or try to walk by holding onto furniture, and strengthen hip and leg muscles to get ready for walking.
pull your baby to standing and hold his arms up to help him walk (but don't do this often, because he needs to stand and strengthen muscles on his own)	"Look at you! "You're walking!"	develop strong muscles, balance, and confidence.

Balance Skills

A young baby might…

- Prefer to play on her belly instead of her back, and lift her head to look around.

- Prop up on one arm and touch objects with the other hand.

- Push up to balance on her hands and knees.

- Get into a sitting position and then fall backward.

- Like to be carried, facing forward in your arms.

- Roll from back to front and from front to back.

- Sit with support.

An older baby might…

- Change from lying facedown to sitting.

- Sit on his own.

- Crawl.

- Balance while rocking back and forth on her hands and knees.

- Sit and play with objects without falling over.

- Get into a kneeling position.

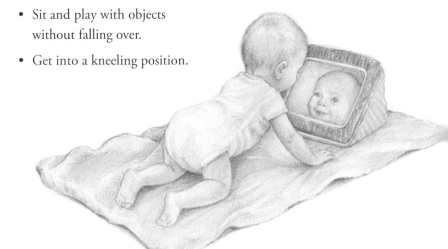

Promoting Your Baby's Balance Skills		
If you…	and say…,	your child will begin to…
take your baby for walks in a stroller, moving quickly and then slowly	"Look! We're going fast!"	look around, and control his head and improve balance and muscle control.
place your baby on her stomach, on a 26-inch or larger ball. Hold her hips securely as you slowly roll the ball backward and forward, and side to side. Repeat the activity with your baby on her back	"Now you're moving forward." "Now you're moving backward."	develop strength and control her muscles, and develop balance by moving against gravity.
place your baby on his back and gently move one leg across his body to help him roll to his belly	"Can you roll to your tummy?"	control and strengthen his muscles, and control his head as he moves from his back to his side to his stomach.
repeat balance activities many times each day and make a daily routine	"Do you remember doing this?"	develop physical skills by doing the activity again and again.
sit your baby on a 10-inch or larger rubber ball and hold her middle as she gently bounces up and down	"Look! You're bouncing!"	develop and strengthen her stomach and upper body muscles, and balance on a moving object.

Ball Skills

A young baby might…

- Hold an object in one hand.
- Hold small objects with the thumb and index finger.
- Show an interest in small objects.
- Hold a ball and drop it.

An older baby might…

- Release a small ball into the air.
- Hold two objects, one in each hand.
- Collect objects and drop them in a basket.
- Tap a beach ball into the air with her feet and hands while lying on her back.
- Sit and roll a ball back and forth with you.

Promoting Your Baby's Ball Skills

If you…	and say…,	your child will begin to…
provide different objects for your baby to grasp and touch, such as a basket with small balls or beanbags	"Can you get the ball?" "Can you put the balls in the basket?"	strengthen his finger and hand muscles, let go of an object and see how it moves, and learn about cause and effect.
drop a beach ball to your child while she's lying on her back	"Can you kick the ball with your feet?"	follow an object through the air, and get body parts ready to hit objects.
sit across from your baby with your legs straight out and roll a 10-inch ball to him	"Push the ball back to me."	learn that balls and other round objects roll, learn to push a ball to make it move, and learn about cause and effect.
stand your baby next to the couch so she can hold onto it, and put a light ball in front of her feet	"I'll show you how to kick the ball." "Can you kick the ball hard?"	strengthen her leg muscles, and balance while lifting one foot to strike the ball.

Your Baby Moves and Learns All Day Long

What's a baby's day like? Much of it is spent being diapered, taking naps, getting dressed, and being fed and bathed. Your baby is exploring and learning the many different things he can do with his body. That means your baby's busy day of routines is your busy day, too. You might be thinking, "There's no time to do anything extra!" However, daily routines are perfect times to play games with your baby and help him understand how his body moves.

Very young children learn from the important adults in their lives. That means you! Every daily routine gives you a chance to talk and play with your baby. Your baby learns to trust and feel safe with you. As your baby learns new physical skills and takes part more and more in daily routines, she develops a sense of all the things she can do.

So while you diaper, bathe, feed, and dress your baby, talk and play with him. Use movement words and play physical games to help him develop physical skills. Tickle his toes, play peek-a-boo, blow bubbles, and roll a ball to him. Don't worry if your baby does not respond to everything you say and do. He is learning from the tone of your voice and the looks on your face. Over time, your baby will get used to your being physically active with him, and he will begin to learn and develop new physical skills.

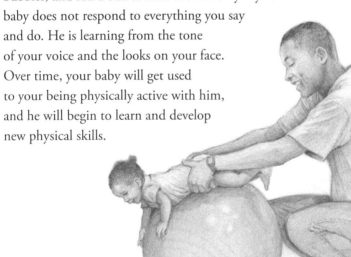

Giving Your Toddler or 2-Year-Old a Good Start

My toddler is full of energy! She crawls up stairs, climbs on chairs, and is walking and even running. She falls a lot but gets up quickly and moves off again. She loves to play with balls.

Toddlers and twos are always moving. They are exploring and trying all the different ways their bodies can move. Daily play will help her develop physical skills. She has gone from crawling to walking to running. She stands on one foot with your help, and she enjoys walking on tiptoes. She travels up and down stairs without holding onto the railing. She walks backward and sideways and loves to climb. Your toddler wants to jump off everything. When your child jumps and lands on two feet without falling, this means she is beginning to understand this basic skill. After jumping, her favorite activities may be with balls.

Your child is learning important physical skills. Now he can move in different directions and can follow different lines drawn on the ground. He loves shaking noisemakers and making sounds by hitting pots with wooden spoons. Even though he may not always do a skill the "right" way, he loves moving and being physically active! It's a fun part of his day. Your toddler is beginning to try balancing and rolling on his own, but he may need your help with these activities. He needs time for daily play, both indoors and outside. He plays hard for 10–15 minutes, but then he wants a short rest before moving again. He sometimes wants to play alone, and at other times he asks you to play with him. Physical activity is at the center of your toddler's life! Each day he is gaining new skills and confidence.

Ways Your Toddler or 2-Year-Old Moves

A toddler might…

- Watch moving objects.

- Listen to songs about the body ("Head, Shoulders, Knees and Toes!"), and touch different body parts along with music.

- Play with different shapes and put all the square shapes in a box.

A 2-year-old might…

- Crawl through tunnels, go over and under low obstacles, and move quickly up and down ramps.

- Use several empty boxes to make an obstacle course.

- Move forward, backward, and sideways.

- Hit a drum both hard and softly and say, "I make music!"

Ways Your Toddler or 2-Year-Old Moves		
If you…	and say…,	your child will begin to…
blow bubbles toward your child	"Can you reach up and touch the bubbles?"	learn about pathways in space by watching bubbles move slowly; get ready to catch an object when she's older.
set up a course at home for your child to move through tunnels and climb over and under obstacles	"Climb through the box! Can you go fast?" "Go around the can."	understand the ideas of *through, fast, over, under, around,* and *slow.*
draw straight, curved, and zigzag lines with colored chalk on the sidewalk	"Can you walk forward and backward on the lines?"	understand the concepts of a path and direction.
say rhymes and sing songs that help your child identify body parts	"My head, my shoulders, my knees, my toes"	learn the words for different parts of the body.

Traveling Skills

A toddler might…

- Move on hands and knees or on his belly, pretending to be an animal. He might slither like a snake or stomp like an elephant.
- Explore walking forward, backward, and sideways.
- Want to hold your hand when walking on a beam or curb.
- Spend time walking on tiptoes.
- Get stuck when climbing and need help getting down.

A 2-year-old might…

- Begin to understand the idea of starting with one foot in order to gallop.
- Run quickly for short distances.
- Jump down from one step but lose balance when landing.
- Begin to pedal ride-on toys.

Promoting Your Toddler's or 2-Year-Old's Traveling Skills		
If you...	and say...,	your child will begin to...
find a playground slide with a short ladder	"Climb the ladder like a firefighter."	not be afraid of heights, climb, and develop strong arm muscles.
provide your toddler with two wooden drum sticks and listen to music together	"Hit the sticks. Follow the beat!" "Raise your knees high as we march to the beat."	develop an awareness of rhythm, and learn how to march by raising his knees high and swinging his arms.
hold your child's hand and gallop around trees in the park	"Take a big step forward!" "Keep that foot in front of you as we move."	practice galloping, leading with one foot forward.
give your child a jumping task and describe his movements out loud	"Jump over the rope and try to land on two feet." "Jump off with two feet and land on two feet." "Swing your arms forward when you jump." "Try to land without falling over."	learn how to jump, land on two feet, and stay balanced when landing.
encourage your child to move in many different ways	"Can you hop like a bunny?" "Can you move slowly like an elephant?"	learn about running, jumping, and walking in different ways.

Balance Skills

A toddler might…

- Pull himself up to stand.
- Stay balanced while she kneels and turns her head.
- Fall frequently when walking or running.

A 2-year-old might…

- Lie on his back and rock back and forth, holding his knees to his chest.
- Jump; attempt to turn in the air; and say, "I can spin!"
- Walk forward and sideways on a beam with some support.
- Balance on different body parts, such as both knees and one elbow, or both hands and one foot.

Promoting Your Toddler's or 2-Year-Old's Balance Skills

If you...	and say...,	your child will begin to...
put your child's feet and hands in the air to round his back (or have him pull his knees to his chest and hold them with his hands)	"Can you rock back and forth?"	learn to make rounded shapes with his body so later he will have an easier time doing forward rolls.
give your child a balancing task and describe her movements out loud	"Move across the beam." "Hold your arms straight out to the side!" "Look forward."	learn to walk across the beam without falling.
help your child pretend to be a statue	"Hold your statue very still." "Make a statue with a wide shape." "Now make one with a narrow shape."	learn to balance while remaining still.
help your toddler stand on one foot by putting one of his hands on a wall and having him hold one foot in the air	"Wow, you're standing on one foot!" "Now try standing on the other foot."	strengthen muscles used for balance, and learn to balance on a small base.
provide riding toys with and without pedals, then give your child a gentle push and let her do all the work	"Place your feet on the pedals. Push down and forward to make the bike move."	control her balance and strengthen her leg muscles.

Ball Skills

A toddler might…

- Grab and release a ball.
- Toss or drop a ball or beanbag into a basket.
- Catch a rolled ball by trapping it with his arms, hands, and body.

A 2-year-old might…

- Kick a ball forward.
- Throw a ball overhand without a targeted direction.
- Attempt to catch a ball by extending her arms directly in front of her body. She may or may not be able to catch the ball.
- Hit a beach ball in the air with his hands.

Promoting Your Toddler's or 2-Year-Old's Ball Skills		
If you…	and say…,	your child will begin to…
sit on the floor with your child and lightly roll balls with different textures, colors, and sizes back and forth	"Let's make this ball roll!"	grab and release a ball and learn to track it as it rolls.
give your child a beach ball to play with and describe his movements out loud	"Can you hit the ball into the air with your hands (head, elbow, feet)?" "Watch the ball as it moves in the air."	track the ball in the air, get his body and hands ready to hit, and swing his arms through a full range of motion to hit the ball.
encourage your child to kick balls that are different sizes and made of soft material	"Put one foot next to the ball. Kick with the other foot as hard as you can!"	develop a full range of motion with the kicking leg, make contact with a ball that sits in place, and look at the ball when kicking.
stand 3–4 feet away from your child and throw a ball to her to catch	"Hold your arms out. When I toss you the ball, wrap your arms around it and catch it."	learn to watch an object and get her body ready to catch it.
put a large target outdoors for your child to hit with a beanbag, focusing on throwing in a forward direction	"Try to hit the target with the beanbag. Throw it as hard as you can!"	learn basic throwing skills by moving the throwing arm through a full range of motion, and build confidence in throwing skills.

Your Toddler or 2-Year-Old Moves and Learns All Day Long

The world is an exciting place for toddlers. Think about all the things you do with your toddler every day. There are routines like diapering and learning to use the toilet, dressing, napping, bathing, and eating. There are daily activities like shopping, going to the doctor, taking walks and rides, playing in the park, and visiting family and friends.

These are all great times to build your relationship with your child and help her learn about the ways her body moves. Remember that much of your child's learning comes from talking and playing with you. When you take a walk together, move and dance to music, throw or kick a ball, and use movement words, you help her learn about all the things her body can do. As you jump over cracks in the sidewalk, talk about what you are doing. When you climb on the jungle gym at the playground, talk about how you are moving. When you move your body to music, talk about how good it feels to move! Think out loud as you use physical skills to solve problems and move from place to place during the day.

Help your 2-year-old pretend! Pretend, or make-believe, play is one of the most important ways children learn about the world and relationships with people. When children pretend during physical play, they learn about people, how objects are used, and ways to make things happen. For example, when children make believe that they are firefighters, they practice skills for climbing ladders and moving quickly. When they pretend to be various animals, children gain strength and control as they move in different ways. Pretending helps children understand that physical activity is an important and fun part of each day.

Giving Your Preschool Child a Good Start

My preschool child is very active! He loves outdoor play and can ride a tricycle and catch a large ball. He can do many things with his body and asks many questions. He does lots of things on his own, like running, galloping, jumping, kicking, and throwing, but he has some difficulty skipping, rolling, and hitting a ball with a paddle or bat. He is certainly learning much about what he can do with his body. How can I help him improve his physical skills?

Your preschool child is learning a lot at school or child care, but you are still his best and most important teacher! The preschool years can be exciting for you and your child. Make the most of this time. Play and be physically active with your child every day.

Think about all the physical things children can do when they are 3, 4, and 5 years old. They run, jump, and leap, and some 5-year-olds even skip. Preschool children show increased balance and control of their bodies. They are able to roll, throw, catch, kick, punt, dribble, and hit a ball. They need your help to get better at these basic skills. Preschool children also have improved fine-motor skills and can put together simple puzzles. They can also hold crayons and pencils and paint brushes, and they can shape clay without help. They are also learning how to use their fingers to move zippers up and down and to button and unbutton things.

Your child is a little ball of energy and looks for active games to play. She is learning fast, so give her at least one but preferably several hours each day to practice the wonderful skills she has learned. This daily physical activity will give your child the skills and confidence she will need as she plays games with friends and peers. The more chances for physical play you can give your child, the more her skills will improve. However, preschool children often tire easily, so make sure your child gets rest periods during physical activity.

Ways Your Preschool Child Moves

A preschool child might…

- Run around trees without bumping into them.
- Draw lines on a piece of paper and then move in those ways—along straight, curved, and zigzag paths; traveling forward, backward, and sideways.
- Place his body at high, middle, and low levels on playground equipment.
- Make narrow, wide, round, and twisted shapes with his body.
- Move fast or slowly when running, galloping, and rolling.
- Play leading and following games (like "tag") with her peers.
- Kick a ball low on the ground or up in the air

Ways Your Preschool Child Moves		
If you...	and say...,	your child will begin to...
challenge your child to walk around your home without touching any people and objects	"Can you touch an object or a person? Then you are too close! Move away!"	move safely without bumping into objects or people, and understand the concept of personal space.
have your child make different shapes with his body	"Make your body tall! Stretch your hands up to the sky!" "Make a round shape, like a ball."	learn body parts and understand how to make shapes with his body.
watch your child move on a playground and describe her movements out loud	"Get down low and crawl under the beam." "Climb high to the top of the ladder." "Can you climb to a middle level?"	understand moving to high, middle, and low levels, and strengthen muscles used in climbing.
give your child a ball and make a tunnel by standing with your feet wide apart	"Can you roll the ball between my legs?" "How high can you throw the ball?"	learn how balls can travel at different levels (low on the ground and high through the air).
play a game of follow-the-leader with your child, changing direction, paths, and speeds	"Can you do what I do? Now it's your turn!"	lead and follow, understand that tag involves running toward and away, and learn to change direction or speed quickly.

Traveling Skills

A preschool child might…

- Jump over each crack on the sidewalk.
- Jump off a low step and shout, "Watch me fly!"
- Jump over objects and land without falling, saying, "Watch how high I can jump."
- Jump and land in different patterns, like hopscotch.
- Play "Follow the Leader".
- March and gallop to the beat of music.
- Gallop, using a broomstick as a horse.
- Race a friend across the playground.

Promoting Your Preschool Child's Traveling Skills

If you…	and say…,	your child will begin to…
place a rope or a hoop on the ground for your child to jump over	"Bend your knees and squat like a frog." "Swing your arms in front of you and up. Now jump!" "Put out your arms when you're in the air. Land with your feet apart."	learn basic jumping patterns, land safely, and maintain balance.
show your child how to gallop and, as you both make movements, describe them out loud	"Take a big step forward. Keep that foot in front of you. Now move forward by stepping with the front foot. Bring the back foot forward."	learn and practice the skill of galloping.
take your child outside to practice running and describe the movements out loud	"Bend your elbows and swing your arms when you run." "How far we can run in 20 seconds?"	discover that he can run faster by bending his elbows and swinging his arms.
play upbeat music and provide your child with musical instruments like bells, rhythm sticks, and drums	"Hit the sticks together to the beat. Raise your knees high and swing your arms as we march along."	practice the skill of marching, learning to raise her knees high when marching to the beat of music.

Balance Skills

A preschool child might...

- Place his hands on the floor; hold one leg in the air; and say, "I'm a statue!"

- Turn a simple walk down the street into an Olympic event by walking and balancing on sidewalk lines and low walls.

- Make the world a balance beam by walking forward, sideways, and backward on objects that are off the ground.

- Extend her arms to the side when walking on a beam.

- Roll down a grassy hill and say, "Here I come!"

- Hold her arms out to the side for balance when hopping on one foot.

Promoting Your Preschool Child's Balance Skills

If you…	and say…,	your child will begin to…
have your child walk across a balance beam	"Step up onto the end of the beam. Step with one foot and then step with the other foot. Hold your arms out like airplane wings!"	learn and refine the skills of walking and balancing on a beam.
give your child activities that encourage balancing on body parts, starting with wide bases of support and progressing to small bases of support	"Balance on three body parts: two elbows and one knee." "Can you balance on one foot?" "Now see whether you can hold that position for 3 seconds without moving!"	keep control of her body, find out how to balance on different body parts, and hold a body position without moving.
have your child practice rolling like a log on a flat surface or on a grassy hill and describe his movements out loud	"Put your legs together. Keep your arms at your side. Turn over slowly and roll down the hill. Go slowly, so you can turn your whole body at the same time."	learn the skill of rolling sideways, maintaining control of his body as he moves.

Ball Skills

A preschool child might…

- Throw a ball; look around to see where it landed; and ask, "Where did it go?"

- Move close to a target when throwing, in order to be successful.

- Stand and kick a stationary ball 10 feet or more, saying, "I'm playing soccer!"

- Run to kick a stationary ball, shouting, "Look how far I can kick!"

- Kick with the toe of her shoe rather than the inside of her foot.

- Dribble a ball with the tips of his fingers.

- Hit a light ball in the air with a paddle three times in a row and then ask, "Will you play tennis with me?"

- Bounce a ball on the floor and then catch it.

Promoting Your Preschool Child's Ball Skills		
If you…	and say…,	your child will begin to…
hang a target on a wall and have your child throw a beanbag at it	"How many times can you hit the target?"	develop throwing skills, throw at a specific target, and develop accuracy.
give your child different soft rubber balls to kick and help her kick with the inside of her foot (not her toe)	"Kick the ball hard! How far does it go?"	kick balls of different sizes and weights, learning proper form and control by kicking with the inside of the foot.
give your child a 10-inch rubber ball to practice catching and dribbling	"Can you drop and catch the ball?" "Can you dribble the ball as you walk forward?"	bounce, catch, and learn how to dribble a ball.
give your child a light ball to hit back and forth with you, first with her hands and then with a light stick or paddle	"Hit the ball back to me. Keep your eye on it so you will know when to hit it."	hit a light ball with her hands, a paddle, or a stick, preparing her body to hit an object.
give your child a light ball to catch	"Toss the ball in the air. When it comes down, try to catch it. Clap your hands around the ball."	practice and develop catching skills, getting his hands and body ready to catch, and watching the ball as it travels through the air.

Your Preschool Child Moves and Learns All Day Long

Your preschool child is learning all the time. You can teach him many things about physical activity by practicing and talking about what you see and do together.

Think about all the things you and your child do every day. Whether at home, in the yard, at the park, or on the playground, you both do physical activity and practice physical skills. Every morning, your child slides out of bed and begins her daily routine of finding different ways to travel through her world. She travels up and down steps, marches, gallops, hops, and runs. She goes over, under, around, and through. She follows different paths, goes in many directions, and changes speeds. There are daily balancing acts to be practiced! Your child plays with different sizes, weights, and colors of balls in order to throw, catch, kick, and hit. Every time she practices a physical skill, your child gets the chance to improve her skills and confidence.

What physical activities can you point out and talk about when you and your child are taking a walk or playing at the playground? How about when you are riding in a car, on a subway, or on a bus? Ask your child which activities he likes most and which he thinks he is the best at doing. Point out physical activities going on around you: adults pushing baby strollers, lifting heavy boxes, and mowing the grass. You might also see people playing soccer, jogging, biking, swimming, dancing, playing tennis, and ice skating. Each physical activity gives you and your child a chance to talk about moving, traveling, balancing, ball skills, and how people use physical skills every day.

Don't forget make-believe play! Many preschool children like to pretend that they are baseball players, firefighters, or ballet dancers. They imagine themselves in the circus, walking across a tightrope. Sometimes they are underground explorers crawling through a cave. Many preschool children like to kick a ball in the yard and call it soccer; shoot a ball in a trash can and call it basketball; hit a ball with a stick or paddle and call it tennis; or swim across the pool and say, "Look! I can swim like my mom and dad!" These important activities help your child develop physical skills. When preschool children use make-believe, they are developing the physical skills and confidence they need to enjoy participating in all types of physical activities.

Ready for Kindergarten

All the time you have spent being physically active with your child has given him the basic skills needed to be healthy throughout his life. Even though he will need more practice, your child now feels confident! He can walk, run, jump, gallop, balance, throw, catch, kick, and hit a ball. Your child knows his body and understands the ideas of direction, path, and level. He has a good understanding of movement and can move safely without bumping into people or objects. He can march, run, and gallop, and he uses those skills without thinking about how he does them. Your child can jump and land without falling. He explores the different ways his body can move. He can balance on low objects and kick a ball hard to make it travel far. He can dribble a ball several times in a row, sometimes while walking. He can watch a ball fly through the air and hit it with his hands, a stick, or a paddle. He is beginning to jump in the air to catch a ball and land on two feet. He's learned a lot about physical activity.

You've had fun, too! You've learned that it is not as hard as you once thought to be physically active every day. Physical activity is all around us and in most of what we do. Your efforts have helped your child explore her world. Physical activity has been good for her, and it has made your bond with your child stronger. So don't stop now. Your child needs your continued help in using physical activity to learn about what you both see, hear, and do. She needs you to point out how physical skills involve different movements and how skills can be put together to play games. She needs lots of opportunities to practice physical skills every day.

Talking With Your Child's Teacher

Show your child's teacher that you care about your child's physical skill learning. Ask when physical activity time is each day and what physical skills are being taught. Find out what skills your child likes to use at school and whether there are any areas in which he needs more help. Tell the teacher what you already do at home to support your child's physical development. Ask what else you can do. Request that regular physical skill instruction take place in your child's school. Remember, when home and school are connected in helpful and respectful ways, children feel more secure. When children feel secure, they are more likely to feel confident about themselves as learners.

Staying Involved

Children who are physically active at school and at home grow into adults who love daily physical activity. They understand that being active leads to healthy lives. It's important that you participate in a variety of physical activities involving the whole family. Invite other children and parents to play! Make sure your child understands how important it is to go outside and play every day. Visit your child's school and get to know his teacher. As a parent, take an active role to make sure physical activity is part of your child's education.

Most of all, have fun and enjoy playing with your child. Be physically active with your growing child every day. Talk about space, paths, high and low, speeds, and making shapes with her body. Enjoy using movement while practicing physical skills. Run, jump, throw, catch, and kick with your child. These skills will lead to the games, sports, and recreational activities she will play when she gets older. Teach your child the importance of physical activity. Physical activity is fun!

Space and Equipment for You and Your Child

Large, open spaces give your child room to repeat activities and practice skills successfully. Even if you don't have a lot of space at home, you can find places where your child can play daily and be physically active. You may need to rearrange chairs and tables so your child has room to move. Visit parks and playgrounds whenever possible. Grassy areas are great for rolling and running!

Of course your child's safety while playing is very important. Whether indoors or out, make sure the spaces are safe. They must be free of dangerous objects, clean, and neat. Outside, make sure your child has space to run, gallop, throw, and kick without bumping into things.

Like learning to read, write, or do math, physical activity often requires some equipment. Having the right kind of equipment helps your child develop and learn about physical skills. Make sure the equipment is soft, light, and made for your child's age and size. You do not have to buy a lot, as many items around your home will work! Physical activity equipment can be used in different ways by babies, toddlers, and preschool children. However, using adult sports equipment that is too large and heavy can make it harder to learn new skills.

Here are some ideas for simple equipment:

- Give your child balls of different sizes, shapes, and weights. They can be made of any safe material, such as foam, plastic, or rubber. You can purchase beach balls and tennis balls or make balls from yarn or socks. You can also make your own beanbags or fill cloth pouches with rice.

- Provide bats, sticks, and paddles to use with balls and beanbags. Make a target by painting a paper plate and hanging it on a wall, fence, or tree.

- Make a tunnel by cutting holes in a large cardboard box or by opening both ends.

- Provide balancing equipment, such as by securely raising a 4- to 6-inch-wide piece of lumber. Make sure that the beam is less than 8 inches off the ground.

- Offer scarves and dance together when the radio is playing. Musical instruments are a wonderful way to encourage eye-hand coordination and small-muscle control.

- Try to provide wheeled vehicles such as tricycles, toy cars, and scooters. Always have your child wear a helmet when using wheeled equipment.

- Use the swings, slides, and climbing equipment in a community park.

Although simple equipment encourages your child to discover new ways of moving and to practice new skills, your involvement is even more important. By continuing to be physically active with your child, you are teaching skills and healthy habits that will last a lifetime!